The Tao of Pug

VIKING STUDIO
Published by the Penguin Group
Penguin Group (USA) Inc., 375 Hudson Street, New York, New York 10014, U.S.A.
Penguin Books Ltd, 80 Strand, London WC2R 0RL, England; Penguin Books Australia
Ltd, 250 Camberwell Road, Camberwell, Victoria 3124, Australia; Penguin Books
Canada Ltd, 10 Alcorn Avenue, Toronto, Ontario, Canada M4V 3B2; Penguin Books
India (P) Ltd, 11 Community Centre, Panchsheel Park, New Delhi – 110 017, India;
Penguin Books (N.Z.) Ltd, Cnr Rosedale and Airborne Roads, Albany, Auckland, New
Zealand; Penguin Books (South Africa) (Pty) Ltd, 24 Sturdee Avenue, Rosebank,
Johannesburg 2196, South Africa

Penguin Books Ltd, Registered Offices: 80 Strand, London WC2R 0RL, England

First published in 2003 by Viking Studio, a member of Penguin Group (USA) Inc.

1 2 3 4 5 6 7 8 9 10

Translation of Tao-te Ching by J. H. McDonald

CIP data available

ISBN 0-670-03258-1

This book is printed on acid-free paper. ∞

Printed in the United States of America
Set in Kennerley
Designed by Jaye Zimet

For Catherine

Introduction

Hello. My name is Wilson the Pug. Long long ago, around 500 B.C., my greatest great grandfather Pug-tzu was living a simple life in China. Along about the same time, a wise old Chinese philosopher known as Lao-tzu was living in the same small village. One day, Lao-tzu happened upon grandpa Pug-tzu in an open field, of which there were many at the time. Lao-tzu had been puzzling for days over some philosophical questions.

When he came upon Pug-tzu, the philosopher put a question to him: "Oh little pug-nosed dog," he said, "how can *this* seem true, but *that* also seem true?"

Pug-tzu stared at Lao-tzu for a moment, then cocked his head to the side as pugs are wont to do.

"Of course!" Lao-tzu exclaimed. "You are so right, little dog. *'True sayings seem contradictory.'*" The old man quickly scribbled the insight onto some silk he was carrying, and with this the Tao-te Ching, the ancient Chinese book of wisdom, was born.

Lao-tzu and Pug-tzu became fast friends and constant companions. Taking his cues from Pug-tzu, the wise old philosopher transcribed the eternal wisdom of the Tao (pronounced like "dow," which rhymes with "cow") into the Tao-te Ching. "Tao" means the way of all life. "Te" means the best use of life. And "ching" means classic text.

Everyone has always wondered what inspired Lao-tzu to write the Tao-te Ching. For centuries, its conception has remained shrouded in mystery and speculation. According to the Tao-te Ching, "The tao that can be described is not the eternal Tao." Words alone are not enough to capture its spirit. So while Lao-tzu was busy writing the Tao-te Ching, Pug-tzu embodied the Tao, right down to the tip of his curly tail, and passed its wisdom down from pug to pug to pug. And now I'd like to share a little of that wisdom with you.

In the pages that follow, I will illustrate the timeless principles of the Tao-te Ching using eighty-one photos—the same number of chapters as in Lao-tzu's classic text—from my very busy life. Each photo is accompanied by a quotation from the Tao-te Ching (with its chapter number in parentheses) along with my own insights and interpretation of the lesson it imparts.

Like you, I have many concerns, daily stresses, and conflicts. Some are even a matter of life and death. On my block alone, there's a German shepherd who'd like to churn me into a finely mashed pug paste. How do I cope? you ask. Well, in the words of the Tao-te Ching, "To those who are good he treats as good. To those who aren't good he also treats as good. This is how he attains true goodness." The Tao reminds me to keep it all in perspective.

So I invite you to suspend what you think you know about scholarly wisdom and talking pugs and go with the flow. As it is written, "Renounce knowledge and your problems will end."

—Wilson the Pug
Berkeley, California

The Tao of Pug

When people see things as beautiful . . .

When people tell me, "You are the cutest thing," I don't get too excited.

After all, other people say pugs are ugly. Either way, it doesn't really matter to me.

Cute and ugly are just opposites that people made up. In the Tao, there are no opposites.

A pug is a pug is a pug. I'm just me, Wilson the Pug. And I'm okay with that.

Heaviness is the basis of lightness.

(26)

Since heavy and light are just more
opposites, I am always the ideal weight.

Long and short define each other.

(2)

See what I mean? More opposites.

Long or short, it doesn't matter. It's all good.

When people see things as good . . .

Sometimes people say,
"Well, aren't you just a little angel!"

. . . evil is created. (2)

Yes, I even help out around the house.

Good or evil,

who can really say which is which?

When his work is done . . .

I chew new life into old shoes.

. . . he takes no credit.
That is why it will last forever. (2)

But with or without my help,
these Birkenstocks will last forever,
just like the Tao itself.

I admit it, sometimes I like to pretend I am a giant ant.

Remembering that I am a role model for my nephew, A-Pug-To-Be-Named-Later,
I return to imparting the simple wisdom of the Tao. And I never let him catch me wearing my giant ant hat.

Some are meant to lead, and others are meant to follow. (29)

A-Pug-To-Be-Named-Later learns the ways of the Tao by following me around,

just as pugs first followed Pug-tzu around.

He is there to help all of creation, and doesn't abandon even the smallest creature.

(27)

This is my very good friend Theodore. Here, I am teaching him to swim. Theodore is too small and legless to fend for himself. So I take care of my little friend just as the Tao takes care of all things.

To those who are good he treats as good.

When Gabriel the cat is nice to me, I'm nice right back.

To those who aren't good he also treats as good. This is how he attains true goodness. (49)

When Gabriel goes a little insane, no matter. I am still nice to him. Sometimes cats can get a bit wacky. But we're both being true to our nature. And this is true goodness.

Fred the turtle is fearless. That is why he never runs away.

I do my best to live in harmony with nature,

so I don't mess with Fred—as much as I might like to.

Find that greatness in the small. (63)

My big friend Henry the coonhound finds
greatness by hanging around with someone
much smaller than he is. And I find greatness
in Henry for not swallowing me whole.

**It dulls the sharp,
unties the knotted . . .**

No matter how hard I pull on the ends of the
rope, the knot remains. But if I leave it alone
and forget about it, the knot and rope both
disappear. And the tomato vine in our
garden is suddenly tied to a pole. The Tao
works in mysterious ways.

. . . shades the lighted . . .

A good pair of sunglasses protects my rather
prominent eyes, just as the Tao protects my
inner vision.

. . . and unites all of creation with dust. (4)

Both the dust bunny and I seek to unite with all creation by uniting with each other.

**When a foolish person hears
of the Tao, he laughs out loud
at the very idea. (41)**

Inside the bag, I am laughing my head off.

**If he didn't laugh,
it wouldn't be the Tao.** (41)

I love to make people laugh. A day without
making people laugh is like a day without
chewing a pig's ear.

I will continue to practice the art of not-doing until I have it perfected.

What, me worry?

Movement overcomes the cold . . .

I run at dawn to heat things up.

It works every time—chilly mornings always give way to warmer afternoons.

. . . and stillness overcomes the heat.

(45)

In the warm afternoons,

I just chill with the Tao.

When I let people cradle me, they seem to really relax into it.

And when they put me down, I can return to one of my important spiritual practices.

By living in harmony with the Tao, I don't have to keep reinventing the wheel.

. . . but it is the center hole that allows the wheel to function. (11)

And by sticking my head into the wheel's center hole, I remind myself to stay centered in the Tao.

The possibilities of Tupperware are endless. Virtually indestructible, it is eternal, just like the Tao.

It is easier to carry an empty cup than one that is filled to the brim. (9)

An empty cup can always be filled with bacon or liver or *anything*.

The potential is infinite, like the Tao itself. But a full cup may already be filled with just plain ho-hum kibble.

If too much time is spent cleaning the house . . .

Cleanliness is good, but I'm not obsessive about it.

. . . the land will become neglected
and full of weeds. (53)

Weeds or a lovely clover field—
who can really tell the difference?

The Tao is always as close as my own breath, which happens to be very loud because of my distinctive nose.

So I am constantly reminded of Its presence, as is everyone around me.

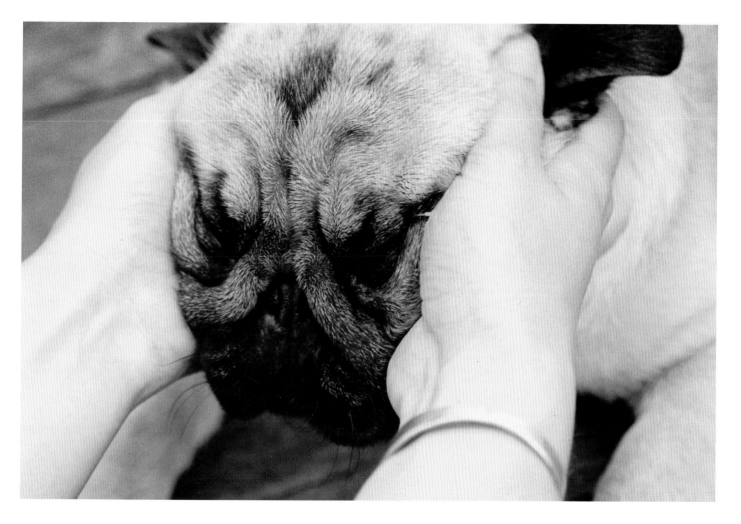

. . . supple as a newborn baby? (10)

I am very supple, as people love to demonstrate.

Without unity, the sky becomes filthy.

(39)

The sky is the source of my life breath.

How could I ever dirty it up?

The space between Heaven and Earth is like a bellows. (5)

Just as the bellows expands and contracts to blow fire into creation, I blow into the bellows to give it a little extra *oomph*.

Five notes deafen the ear. (12)

Fortunately, there are infinitely more than five notes. When I listen to my favorite song, I can hear the infinity of the Tao.

Let people enjoy the simple technologies. (80)

I whisper the secrets of the Tao to my friend the robot dog.

He has sound sensors, so I know he's taking it all in.

A journey of a thousand miles starts with a single footstep. (64)

Any journey I take usually starts with one footstep into the car. I prefer a fuel cell model.

Fortunately, I can travel without ever leaving my Sherpa bag. That's just how it is with the Tao.

I can venture far and wide but not have to exert too much.

I am also carried in and embraced by my yin-yang bag.

In this way, I achieve true balance.

**The tallest tree begins
as a tiny sprout. (64)**

Big tree or little me, it doesn't matter. The
Tao is in everything great and small.

My toys depend on me to watch over them.

Especially my bunny, who is frequently the target of kidnap attempts.

The Tao teaches us about letting go. I am still learning.

The more wealth you possess,
the harder it is to protect. (9)

Whenever I find money lying on the ground,
I pick it up. This way, I free people from the
temptation to spend it unwisely. The Tao has
a way of keeping everything in balance.

**A good bookkeeper has
an excellent memory. (27)**

I remember to keep track of the money I
find. But truly, the Tao keeps track of all
things.

My friend Frank the Pug has achieved greatness.

Thus he is like the Tao itself.

. . . I alone am dull and uncouth. (20)

I am a simple pug with simple tastes.
But there is greatness in simplicity,
so I too am like the Tao.

**To wear fancy clothes and ornaments,
to have your fill of food and drink
and to waste all of your money buying
possessions is called
the crime of excess.** (53)

I avoid wearing a tuxedo if at all possible.
But on Pugcademy Awards night, when
Frank was nominated for Best Pug in a
Feature Film, I was happy to dress up.

Let them make their own clothes. (80)

I prefer to make my own clothes, like this

hat. In this way, I not only experience

the Tao of creation, but I can also

allow for a nice roomy fit.

As I contemplate ice melting after a barbecue, I'm reminded that things change form
but never disappear entirely. And that *some* puddles cause no problems.

. . . whole as an uncarved block of wood. (15)

The uncarved block is
my role model for wholeness.

We fashion wood for a house . . .

By spending time in the mailbox,

I not only get to contemplate the joy of the sheltering Tao,

but I am also first to receive the mail.

I contemplate this house's emptiness in case
I ever need a change from the mailbox.

The block of wood is carved into utensils by carving void into the wood.

The Master uses the utensils. (28)

The block of wood is carved into a back scratcher.

If I am puzzled by something, I use the back scratcher as a head scratcher

and soon I forget what was puzzling me.

**The more knowledge you seek,
the less you will understand. (47)**

I love books. But since I can't read,
I experience the Tao directly by
contemplating their infinitely varied covers.

Even though the Tao is everywhere,

a dwelling made of pillows is ideally located on the bed.

My door, like the door to the Tao, is always open.

The supreme good is like water. . . .

The fountain of the Tao springs infinite and eternal.

But water is precious, so I savor every drop.

The kitchen sink will never be a popular hangout.

But no matter; the Tao is indeed everywhere.

**When it rains hard,
it lasts but a little while.** (23)

As a big fan of water, I welcome a little hard rain. Sunshine or rain, who can say which is better? Either way, I am certainly glad to have my raincoat.

When the hard rain knocks out the power, I contemplate the dark and mysterious virtue of the Tao.

I am also reminded of the mysterious virtue of electricity.

Yet nothing is better than water
for overcoming the hard and rigid,
because nothing can compete with it.

(78)

I prefer water that is bottled at the source,
since the Tao is the source of all good things.

Do not meddle with people's livelihood. (72)

I have a special way of signaling when I need a break from taking pictures.

By honoring my natural rhythms I am honoring the Tao.

He who follows the way of the Tao will draw the world to his steps. (35)

Every day I eagerly await the arrival of the mailman, who brings news of the world. I am especially thrilled to draw him to my steps for he is a Taoist sage.

It is easy to love the mailman, but how do you learn to love yourself?

I practice on this stuffed pug. I've named him Wilson the Pug. He's okay with that.

When the country falls into chaos . . .

Sometimes I am glad I can't read.

. . . politicians talk about 'patriotism.''

(18)

I am a patriot of all countries. The Tao has
no borders.

Do you want to rule the world and control it? I don't think it can ever be done. (29)

No one can really rule and control the world

any more than I can rule and control this inflatable globe.

After armies take to war,
bad years must always follow. (30)

War is bad for pugs
and for other living things.

I resist the urge to poke the fish.

Sometimes I wish our leaders would resist the urge to poke their fish.

**Those who lead people by following
the Tao don't use weapons to enforce
their will. (30)**

I practice nonviolence by sitting
with these nunchakus but never
actually picking them up.

Sometimes my fishy friend Theodore and I play hide and seek.

I usually let him do the hiding.

. . . it is best to keep weapons

out of sight. (36)

If I keep weapons out of sight,
I find they are quickly out of mind.

Things are easier hid while they are still small. (64)

When Theo lets me hide, he can never find me.

The Tao is hidden yet always present, not unlike the little heart shape on my bottom.

One of my favorite activities is no activity at all.

The name that can be spoken

is not the eternal Name. (1)

Wilson the Pug is my spoken name,

but since I can't actually speak,

I am more in touch with my eternal self.

When people try to name the Tao, they never succeed.

And when people call me "the dog," I don't pay much attention.

The tao that can be described is not the eternal Tao. (1)

So what *is* the Tao? you ask.

Well, I could try to tell you, but then it wouldn't be the Tao.

The Tao is just the Tao. I'm just me, Wilson the Pug. And I'm okay with that.

Acknowledgments

A kind heart makes the giving good. (8)

The authors would like to extend their deepest gratitude and appreciation to the following people. Only by virtue of their kindness was this book made possible.

Stacie Blair of the Pacific Firm for her great flexibility, Eric Burkhart for access to his lovely garden, Mike Daisey for sharing inspiration and his agent, Jean-Michele Daisey, for lending her creative discernment, Iris Davis and Davis Black and White for their artful printing, Beatrice Marot for her keen foresight, Sheira Khan, Michael Robins, and La Marr Desmond Dekker, a very special Rottweiler.

For their graciousness, we thank Columbia Tristar Motion Picture Group, Ted Danson, Fish, Mackenzie Phillips and Lee Allan, NECA, Ben & Jerry's, Crystal Geyser, Birkenstock, Geospace International, Tupperware, Tamara Romijn and Henry, Ann Hart and Gabriel, Myrna Powell and School House Pugs, Rosemary Robles and Pocket Pugs, Lisa Sheeran and Frisco Pugs, Pegasus Fine Books, Photolab, Avi Messeri and Brenda Farmer, and J. H. McDonald for a wonderful translation of the Tao-te Ching.

Special thanks to our editor, Alessandra Lusardi, for her tireless enthusiasm and support, Clare Ferraro for her lucid vision, our publicist Gretchen Koss for her dogged determination, and our agents Arielle Eckstut and Daniel Greenberg of the Levine Greenberg Literary Agency for their patience, wisdom, and trusted counsel.

For inspiring us, we thank the Oakland Athletics and the Grateful Dead.

Last but not least, we thank Nancy's family, her father, the late Irwin Levine, and her mother, Eileen Levine, and her sister Fran Herault for providing strong roots, Wilson's parents Blaze and Heidi for their good genes, and most especially Catherine Woodman who is the sunshine of our lives. Nancy also wishes to thank Wilson the Pug for being such a good sport, not to mention a Taoist master.